CARDIFF

Remember When

BRIAN LEE

CARDIFF
Remember When

For Joan and George Holland
Friends of long standing

First published in Great Britain in 2009 by The Breedon Books Publishing Company Limited, Breedon House, 3 The Parker Centre, Derby, DE21 4SZ.

This paperback edition published in Great Britain in 2013 by DB Publishing, an imprint of JMD Media Ltd

ISBN 978-1-78091-337-7

Printed and bound in the UK by Copytech (UK) Ltd Peterborough

CONTENTS

Author's Acknowledgements

I would like to thank all those who loaned me photographs for this book. These include: Media Wales, Russell Harvey, Alec McKinty, Graham Pritchard, Mr J. Jones, David Davies FRICS, Allen Hambley, Fred Suller, Elizabeth Wilson, Patrick Stephens, House of Fraser, Derek Carder, Mac Beames, John Ruddle, Richard Meade, Pam John and Joan Holland. I would also like to thank those people who loaned me photographs which I was unable to use.

I also want to thank Tony Woolway, chief librarian at Media Wales, and his assistants Edwina Turner and Rob Mager for their help, and Katrina Coopey and her staff at the Cardiff Central Library. If I have inadvertently omitted anyone from these acknowledgements then I apologise.

Foreword

In my thirty plus years as an employee of the *Western Mail and Echo* (now Media Wales), most of which have been spent managing the company's archives, I've had a front-row seat in watching the changes taking place in and around Cardiff. At my fingertips I have what is certainly the largest private photo library in the Principality and, quite often, images are sourced from our vast photographic archive to show sites, landmarks and events long since gone – though in these pictures and in the memories of those old enough to remember, they're certainly not forgotten.

As a Fairwater lad, much that I took for granted as a child has sadly changed or disappeared. Long gone is the Regent cinema where I spent many a Saturday morning, galloping back through Birdies Lane on my way home with my mates to re-enact scenes from the films we'd just seen. As a teen, Saturday afternoons were spent browsing the racks of Buffalo Records in David Morgan's Arcade, to be followed by American Cream Soda with a dollop of ice cream at the Sarsaparilla shop, both sadly gone, as is the Top Rank, a place where I strutted what little stuff I had during some memorable Saturday evenings out on the town.

Fortunately we have Brian Lee on hand to document these changes and events. Many's the time I've had cause to call on Brian's vast knowledge of Cardiff's history, while his books have always been a very good reference source, often jogging memories of a very different era in the growth of the capital city. Long may he continue to publish these interesting and valuable collections.

Tony Woolway

CHAPTER ONE
THE PARK HOTEL

James Howell, the founder of Cardiff's oldest department store, Howells, was the man behind the building of the Park Hotel. He and five or six other local businessmen were responsible for the formation of the Park Hall & Hotel Company Limited in 1882, formed for the purpose of building a 'high class family hotel of 100 bedrooms' on the site of the old theatre in Crockherbtown, now known as Queen Street.

In 1983 the Park Hotel celebrated a century of hospitality, as 1883 was the year that the hotel was granted a licence to sell alcohol. The exact date of opening is not known, but it is thought to have been some time between February and March 1885. It is known that a concert at the Park Hall, which was converted to a cinema in 1916, was fully reported by the local press on 29 April 1885, and an 1886 almanac refers to the Park Hotel building as being 'now completed'.

Said to resemble a 'watered down version of the Louvre in France', the Park Hotel was built on the edge of parkland, where the magnificent civic centre buildings now stand. It housed a number of shops and offices and over the years millions of pounds have been spent on improving this well-known Cardiff landmark. For instance, when Mount Charlotte took over the hotel in 1972 they spent £1.5 million on refurbishment, with

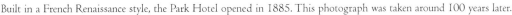

Built in a French Renaissance style, the Park Hotel opened in 1885. This photograph was taken around 100 years later.

The Park Hall dining room in July 1958.

£150,000 of that spent on decorations and furnishings in the Harlech Lounge and Caernarvon Room Restaurant. When general manager Nicholas Menzies told the press in 1986 that 'the hotel is like the Forth Bridge; we never actually finish', he was not joking. The Parc, as it is now known, is continually being updated, yet at the same time still retains its Victorian elegance.

The first major modernisation came in 1935, when the hotel was still rooted deep in the Victorian era, with brass bedsteads and net curtains. This change brought wall-to-wall carpeting, built-in wardrobes and easy chairs, and a writing table in each of its then 115 bedrooms.

Generations of Cardiffians have happy memories of the Park Hotel, with many holding their wedding receptions there. Some couples return years later to celebrate their wedding anniversaries in one of the elegant function rooms. Major refurbishments were made in 1996 when it became the 49th hotel to carry the name of Thistle, the UK's premier hotel group. More than 200 guests from businesses in Cardiff celebrated the relaunch and more improvements were made to the now 136 luxury bedrooms, the oak-panelled Whitehall Suite and the first-floor Princes Suite, both of which provide accommodation for up to 250 people. Marble steps were laid leading to the front entrance, mahogany doors were installed and the reception area and concierge desk completely refurbished.

The saddest day in the history of the hotel was 27 December 2006, when the building was devastated by a massive fire. Fifty firefighters battled the flames and nearly 100 guests had to be evacuated. However, all traces of the devastation have now gone and the hotel has since revealed its new look.

In 1956 the Park Hotel's bar was billed as 'Cardiff's Most Modern Bar.'

A more modern look to the restaurant in February 1963.

The Park Hotel celebrated its centenary in 1983.

The Lord Mayor, Councillor Olwen Watkins (centre), gives a civic send-off to the balloons – each one carrying a guinea birthday voucher – at the hotel's centenary celebrations.

Mr Fred Lewis, who celebrated his 100th birthday in 1983, was treated to a special champagne tea courtesy of the Park Hotel. Ellen John is pictured in period costume, serving Mr Lewis his meal.

According to the *Egon Ronay Lucas Guide* of 1982, the Park Hotel, which had been extensively refurbished, was Wales's top hotel. Manager Mr Christopher Skidmore stands proudly outside his award-winning hotel.

Pictured in the hotel's Caernarvon Room Restaurant are general manager Nicholas Menzies (seated) with some of his young management team. From left: Karen Williams, Peter Ratcliffe, Mark Fulton, Alan Price, Michael Lennon and Doris McIntyre, 1985.

The Park Hotel's newly furbished Harlech Lounge, with its redesigned bar, is seen here in June 1986.

One hundred and twenty full-time staff were employed at the Park Hotel in 1986. The recently refurbished Caernarvon Room Restaurant was designed in a country house style.

CHAPTER TWO
CAPITOL CINEMA

Originally opened in 1921, the Capitol Cinema, or the Cap as it was known to many, entertained generations of Cardiffians until its closure in 1978. Due to its central location and distinctive decor the Capitol was more successful than most cinemas and was often full to capacity. It had an eventful history, and Hollywood stars like Charlton Heston and Danny Kaye visited it to promote their films.

Cardiff's most cherished cinema was the Capitol on Queen Street, which opened in 1921 and closed in 1978. It was demolished to make way for the Capitol Exchange shopping centre. This photograph was taken *c.*1955.

Generations of Cardiffians would meet outside the Capitol Cinema on first dates. The Beatles, Danny Kaye, Shirley Bassey, Tom Jones and Bill Haley and his Comets are just some of the performers who trod the Capitol's boards. The cinema is seen here in 1982.

The balcony at the Capitol Cinema was said to be the largest of its kind in Britain, c.1960.

Mr Alfred Totterdale, who installed the Capitol Cinema's projectors, has one last look before all of the cinema's equipment was auctioned in 1980.

Auctioneer Mr Noel Davies examines the famous Capitol Cinema clock, 1980.

Projectors like these transported thousands of cinema-goers to places all over the world, *c*.1960.

A happy staff function at the Capitol Cinema in January 1938.

Capitol Cinema staff line up for a group photograph to mark the showing of the 1933 film *The Big Broadcast*.

A Capitol Cinema staff get-together in the 1930s. Seated on the extreme right is Miss Kathleen Boghurst, chief cashier, who worked for 13 years in the cinema.

It is hard to believe that this partly demolished building once played host to grand opera and music ranging from Beethoven to The Beatles and was once the finest cinema/theatre in Wales, 1983.

A stark reminder that the proud Capitol Cinema was once situated on this site, 1984.

CHAPTER THREE
PICTURE PALACES OF THE PAST

Many Cardiffians have happy memories of their favourite cinemas, now long since gone. Another Queen Street cinema was the Gaumont, which closed in 1960 and was later demolished to make way for a C&A department store. It had originally opened in 1887 as Levino's Hall and was renamed the Empire Theatre a few years later. It had a sliding roof, which could be opened during the interval to provide theatre-goers with some fresh air. When it was a theatre, the stars of the day, such

Chief of staff at the Gaumont Cinema, Mr G. Murray, stands on the steps for the last time before the cinema closed down in 1960.

Mr John Blagden checks his projector before the last performance at the Gaumont Cinema, 1960. He worked for the Rank Organisation for 50 years.

as Marie Lloyd, Dan Leno, Vesta Tilley, Harry Tate, Albert Chevalier, George Robey and Sir Harry Lauder all trod its boards. In 1913 the world-famous escapologist Harry Houdini performed his Chinese water torture cell routine there, apparently for the first time.

The Olympia, also in Queen Street, opened as Andrews Hall in 1899 and later became the Cannon Cinema in 1986. Yet another Queen Street Cinema was the Queens, which showed the old black and white horror films like *Dracula*, *Frankenstein* and *The Wolf Man*. Today Specsavers is situated there.

Of the local fleapits the grandest was probably the Gaiety Cinema in City Road. Opened in 1912 by the Lord Mayor, it was known as the Grand Gaiety Cinema.

This glittering occasion at the Empire Theatre was the 1950 Royal Command film performance of *The Mudlark*. Included in the line up of front-row stars are Montgomery Clift, Petula Clark, Terry Thomas, Gloria Swanson, Jack Warner, Leslie Mitchell, Beatrice Campbell, Anthony Steel and Richard 'Stinker' Murdoch.

Originally a concert hall, the Park Hall was converted to a cinema in 1916 and closed in 1971.

Opened in 1896 as Andrews Hall, the Olympia became the ABC Queen Street Cinema and later still the MGM. It is seen here *c.*1967.

The MGM Cinema, Queen Street, 1994. In 1976 the cinema had become the first triple screen cinema in Cardiff.

The MGM had reverted to being called the ABC when this photograph was taken in 1999.

Opposite: The Odeon in Queen Street opened as the Imperial Picture Palace in 1911. It became known as the Odeon in 1936, and this photograph was taken in 1962.

Originally a roller-skating rink, the Central Cinema on The Hayes is photographed in the year it closed down, 1959. It was situated where the entrance to Oxford Arcade once stood.

PICTURE PALACES OF THE PAST

The Queen's Cinema opened in 1909 and was demolished in 1955.

Opposite: The Pavilion in St Mary Street opened as the Philharmonic Hall in 1889. It closed in 1968 and became the Gala Bingo and Social Club in 1976.

A view of the Empire Theatre in 1935.

The Empire Theatre became the Gaumont Cinema in 1954 and was demolished in the early 1960s to make way for C&A. It is seen here in 1959.

John Henry 'Harry' North, aged 90, built the 1,228-seater Plaza Cinema in 1928 with his brother Alfred. He is seen here with his wife, Florence, also aged 90, in 1981.

A double bill of X-certificate horror films: *Alien* and *The Fog* were the final films shown at the Plaza Cinema on North Road, Gabalfa, on 17 October 1981.

The Coliseum on Cowbridge Road, Canton. Like many Cardiff cinemas, it ended its days as a bingo hall. It was opened in 1913 and closed in 1959.

The Avenue in Ely, 1961. It opened in February 1940 and closed in June 1960. It later became a bingo hall before making way for a garage and showrooms.

Originally known as the Penylan Cinema in 1910, this building later became the Globe Cinema and when this photograph was taken it was known as La Continentale. It was demolished in 1985 and shops and a small cinema were built on the site.

42nd Street stood on the site of the old Globe Cinema in 1988.

Opened in 1914 as a silent film theatre, the Ninian Cinema in Grangetown had seating for 600 patrons. *HMS Defiant* was showing when this photograph was taken in August 1972, just as it closed.

The Grand Gaiety Cinema on City Road opened in 1912 and closed in 1961.

This was all that was left of the County Cinema on Newport Road in 1986. Opened in 1939, it closed in 1974 and was demolished to build a retirement housing complex.

The Capitol Odeon Cinema, which opened on the corner of Station Terrace and Queen Street in 1992, was the first multiplex cinema in Cardiff. It has since closed.

The New Chapter Arts Centre and Cinema in Canton, November 1974.

The Monico on Pantbach Road, Rhiwbina, opened in 1937 and was demolished in 2003. This photograph was taken in 1979 and a block of luxury flats is now situated on the site.

CHAPTER FOUR
SHOPPING AROUND

Not many cities can boast a shopping area like Cardiff and when the new £675 million St David's 2 development is completed it will be even more progressive. This chapter focuses on the main city centre streets – Queen Street and St Mary Street – but there are several long-forgotten out of town shops, like Hopson & Son Ltd in Albany Road. This was one of the largest retail and wholesale distributing tobacconists in South Wales.

Cardiff was fortunate in possessing a number of first-class departmental stores and David Morgan and James Howell & Co., now part of the House of Fraser group, were two of them. The former sadly disappeared in 2005, but for lovers of fashion the Howells House of Fraser store, which has 100 departments each containing a comprehensive stock of modern merchandise, is still very much with us.

Within the store there is the entrance to a church, the façade of which was retained and lovingly preserved when a new extension was built around the building sometime in the 1960s. The church was called the Bethany Baptist Church and was founded in 1806 when the Revd William Bradley baptised three adults in the nearby River Taff. When workmen were digging trenches on the site in 1964 they discovered 12 skeletons. The store took legal advice and were told that as long as the bones were reverently interred on the same spot there was no need to inform the coroner. Several spirits are said to haunt the store.

To mark the centenary of Howells, a replica of the original James Howell coach and horses visited the Mansion House to deliver a bouquet of flowers to the Lord Mayor, Alderman Mrs Miriam Bryant, in 1965. The Mansion House was built by James Howell in 1896.

Howells – The Harrods of Wales. Wharton Street is to the left of the photograph, which was taken in 1961.

The St Mary Street entrance to Howells, 1972.

When Friday night shopping was introduced in Howells in the 1960s it soon became popular.

Howells closed their food hall in 2008. This photograph was taken 40 years earlier, when the food hall was situated on Wharton Street.

The finely carved pillars in the Wallis fashion department of Howells are all that remain of the Bethany Baptist Church, founded in 1806 and situated near the menswear department, 1984.

When this photograph was taken in 1961, Seccombes on Queen Street were celebrating their 71st birthday.

This photograph shows the frontage of Seccombes in Park Place in 1973. The store closed four years later in 1977.

Another popular Queen Street store was Mackross.

Shoppers wait outside Mackross for the start of the Christmas sales on 29 December 1976.

This Marments store picture was taken in more elegant times and shows the hosiery and glove department, c.1930.

Marments Ltd, Queen Street. The famous Carlton Hotel was to the extreme right of the picture, *c.*1930.

Mrs Maria Davies, who worked on the Marments window and shop displays for five years, emerges from the 1929 lift interior with its oak panelling, 1986.

Everything was up for grabs when Marments closed in 1986, including these 1928 plaster heads from the millinery department.

Calders, on the corner of Queen Street and Churchill Way, opened in 1920 as a gentlemen's outfitters and was expanded in 1975 to include a ladies' fashion section and a coffee lounge. It is seen here in 1981.

British Home Stores, Queen Street, October 1957.

A Wimpy, which used to be on the corner of Queen Street and Charles Street, 1988.

Burger King is now situated where Wimpy once stood, 2000.

Millets Ltd, which was adjacent to Calders on Queen Street, was established in 1928. This picture was taken in August 1969.

British Home Stores opened on the site of the old Carlton Hotel in 1955. Thirty years later, in 1985, the store moved to bigger premises in Queen Street on the site of the former Woolworth store.

The Woolworth store on Queen Street. The modern frontage dated from 1960 and the photograph was taken two years later.

Marks & Spencer, Queen Street. To the right of the photograph can be seen the Taff Vale pub, which stood on the corner of Paradise Place, 1969.

Evan Roberts, which was situated on the corner of Kingsway and Queen Street, in 1984.

C&A stood on the site of the old Gaumont Cinema. The store came to Cardiff in 1963 and closed in 2003.

The notice in the window reads that Masters & Co., Tailors and Outfitters for nearly a century, had acquired these premises. Evan Roberts (left) and Marments (right) stood either side of the building in 1953.

Lermons on The Hayes is another vanished city centre store, seen here in 1960.

How many Cardiffians remember In Gear in the High Street Arcade?

One of Cardiff's best-loved shops was David Morgan, the family store on The Hayes, which closed in 2005.

Toiletries department, David Morgan, 1988.

Linen department, David Morgan, 1988.

The Great British Burger Bar in St David's Centre, 1988. The notice in the window reads 'A delicious free doughnut with filter coffee'.

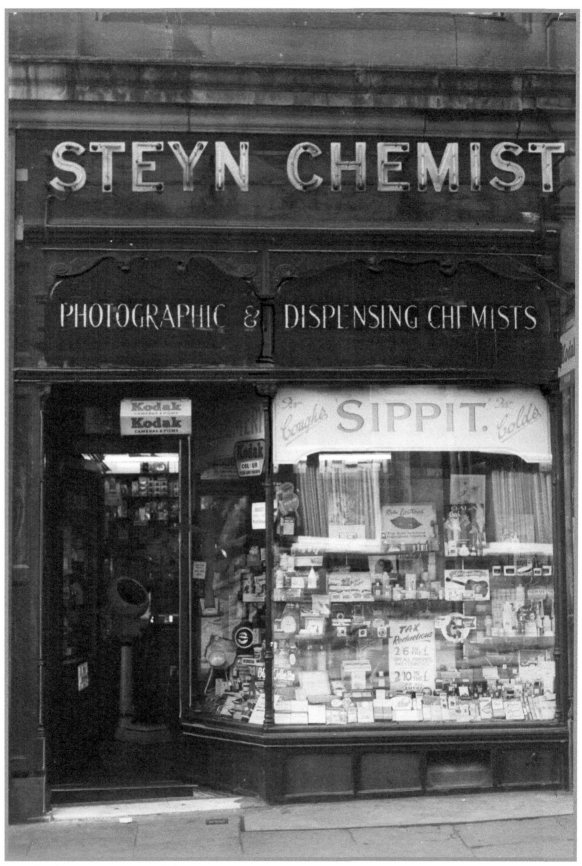

Steyn the Chemist, St Mary Street, 1958.

One of the oldest jewellers in Cardiff was Crouch, who had a shop on St Mary Street for many years. It is seen here *c.*1950.

Robert Dunn, tobacconist, used to be at No. 15 Wharton Street. Miss Abergail Dunn is seen leaving the shop for the last time in 1958 before it was closed down. The shop was later demolished to make way for the Howells extension.

Grimwade's of Canton in 1964. As the notice in the window left of the picture claimed: 'We buy, sell and exchange almost anything in the second-hand world.'

House of Hopson, the tobacconists on Albany Road, seen here in 1967. The business was founded in 1891 by Mr H.A. Hopson.

The front of Gordon E. Cirel Ltd in Wellfield Road, which was broken into by thieves who got away with £7,000 worth of clothes in October 1966.

CHAPTER FIVE
STREET SCENES

A visitor to the town of Cardiff in the early 19th century would have found the debtors' prison, town hall and butter market all situated on the High Street, conveniently close to the old quay (hence Quay Street). The High Street was considered to be the best business street in Cardiff and this so annoyed the tradesmen of Duke Street that in 1829 they issued a broadsheet proclaiming their wares. The landlords of the Olde Green Dragon, the Crown and Anchor, the Three Tuns and the Globe and Shears issued a joint advertisement claiming that the wines and beers at their hostelries were 'the finest in Cardiff' and superior to those inns found on the High Street. The landlord of the Three Tuns also boasted that for the convenience of his patrons a passage led from the Three Tuns to the High Street meat market.

Among the other tradesmen a visitor to Cardiff in 1829 would have found on Duke Street were W. Allen, baker and confectioner, and E. Young, mercers and drapers. Mr D. Evans claimed to sell 'the safest drugs in town', while the best china tea could be obtained from Smith and French the grocers. Other shopkeepers who advertised their wares were C.C. Williams the currier and leather merchant, J. Wheeler the architect and W. Reed, bookbinder, printer and bookseller.

The London to Milford coach used to pass through Duke Street, which in those days was only 14 feet wide in places. It was formerly known as Duck or Shoemaker Street. The sewer system consisted of open gullies and a nearby brook was often polluted by tannery refuse.

As for Queen Street, once known as Crockarton in 1384, Crockerton Street in 1660 and Crockherbtown from 1774 to 1887, people from all over the county would travel there for the horse fair. They would stay in the Old Masons Arms or the Rose and Crown situated on North Street, now Kingsway. Near to here was the old town pound, which had a hole in the wall so that people could see if any of their animals had been impounded. Queen Street was nothing like it is today and one Cardiffian had this to say about the Queen Street house he lived in: 'It had a beautiful, old-fashioned and wonderfully productive garden. I grew figs and mulberries there, and there was mistletoe growing on the apple trees. In those days the theatre stood about where the Park Hotel stands now, and there was a lane known as Bradleys Lane going up where Park Place is now. Mr Bradley's father was a hunting man and had large stables in Womanby Street.'

St Mary Street derives its name from the old parish church of St Mary's, and its name came into being some time at the beginning of the 16th century.

This was Queen Street in June 1969, before it became a pedestrian-only area.

This photograph of Queen Street was taken in the 1970s.

No fumes, no noise and no fear of traffic in Queen Street in 1975.

Littlewoods was a familiar sight in Queen Street for around half a century and employed more than 300 workers. Sadly, the store closed in 1998.

Evan Roberts had a shop on the corner of Park Place and Queen Street when this photograph was taken in January 1962.

Yet another vanished store is Marments, which was situated on the opposite side of the road to Mackross.

Russell Harvey took these photographs of the Queens Arcade shopping centre, which was opened on 28 April 1994.

Mackross, c.1960, another Queen Street store which has long since disappeared.

One way of cleaning the Queens Arcade windows!

The existing St David's Centre and the new £675 million St David's 2 development which, when completed, will link via the former town South Mall.

Another city-centre street which has seen many changes over the years is Charles Street, seen here in 1978.

Charles Street was named after Charles Vachell, who built one of the first houses in Queen Street.

The prize-winning Cardiff in Bloom, St David's Centre, August 1989.

St David's Link shopping arcade c.1987. It was said to be 'an enhancement for the city centre', but was demolished to make way for the St David's 2 development project.

Bakers Oven, like Iceland and the popular Golden Grove bookshop, was demolished to make way for St David's 2.

Iceland, 2004.

The junction of Bridge Street and Hayes Bridge Road, which has since been redeveloped, *c*.1975. The building to the extreme left was the Greyhound public house.

Another part of the city centre which has been redeveloped is Working Street, seen here in 1978.

This photograph was taken in the Hill Street area in 1978. The rear of the Mackross building can be seen to the extreme left of the image.

Siemens and Brown Brothers used to be on the corner of Hills Terrace and Frederick Street. Geoffrey Gee had taken over the Siemens building when this picture was taken in 1978.

Frederick Street looking towards Queen Street, 1978. In the centre can be seen the 25-storey Capital Tower building.

J. Gulliford & Sons, a bookseller which used to be on the corner of Wharton Street and St Mary Street, is seen here in 1951. A Ladbrokes betting shop is now situated on the site.

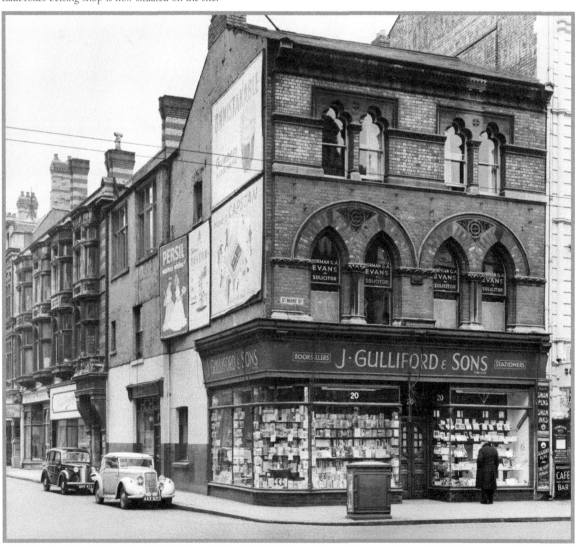

In 1956 Anros the fashion shop was situated at No. 7 High Street.

The James Howell & Co. department store in St Mary Street, which was sold to House of Fraser in 1972.

The canopy of the Queen's Hotel in St Mary Street was demolished when a lorry, pictured right, crashed into it in 1977.

The popular Sandringham Hotel in St Mary Street was known as the Black Lion many years ago. This photograph was taken in 1963.

Hodge House, which was situated on the corner of Guildhall Place and St Mary Street, c.1985.

Barclays Bank, which was also to be found on the other corner of Guildhall Place and St Mary Street, c.1985.

Looking towards Cardiff Castle from the High Street, c.1925.

Magnet House in Kingsway, photographed c.1955. It was demolished some time ago and a new building called 1 Kingsway has since replaced it. Greyfriars Road can be seen to the right of the photograph.

These buildings in the Hill Street area were also demolished to make way for the St David's 2 shopping centre, 2003.

The bus station in Central Square was partly demolished in 2008.

An alternative view of the bus station in 1988 before it was demolished.

CHAPTER SIX
MEMORABLE MOMENTS

Many famous people have visited Cardiff over the years and in this chapter we are reminded of just some of them. Pope John Paul II paid his first papal visit to Wales in 1982, while Nelson Mandela was made a freeman of the city in 1998.

Another famous person to come to Cardiff was Field Marshal Viscount Montgomery, who was carrying out an inspection at the opening of the Douglas Haig Memorial Homes in the Rumney area of the city in 1953.

Cardiff's own characters included late businessman Norman Harvey, who had a notice in his car showroom and garage in Penarth Road which read: 'Keep Clear Of the Lioness'. Sheba, a 10-month-old lioness, who weighed 160lb, spent most of the day padding silently around the garage or perched sleepily on top of a used car. Harry 'Don't Tarry Sell To Harry' Parfitt, who had a scrap metal business in Thesiger Street, is another Cardiff character who stands out. During the 1950s Harry appeared on Eamon Andrews's much-loved television show *What's My Line*.

The controversial Cardiff solicitor Leo Abse is also illustrated in this chapter. It was reported that a roar of laughter went up in the House of Commons during one question time when, on Budget Day 1961, he strode into the chamber wearing a brown Van Dyck stovepipe hat, a stone coloured suit and a sepia waistcoat, while in his buttonhole he wore a brown orchid. The Minister of Labour, Mr John Hare, who was answering questions when Mr Abse entered, joined in the laughter, which continued as Abse crossed the bar of the House and walked almost the full length before taking his seat.

The Prime Minister, the Rt Hon. Harold Macmillan MP, waves to the crowd as he arrives to unveil a statue of David Lloyd George in July 1960. Also seen in the picture is the Lord Mayor, Alderman Mrs Dorothy Lewis, and the chairman of the fund, the Hon. Anthony Berry.

Radio and television personalty Maureen Staffer officially opens the Annual Catholic Fête and Sports Day at Llanrumney Avenue Sports Field, August 1958.

Maureen Staffer goes backstage at the New Theatre for her special Radio Wales New Year's Day programme, 1984.

The controversial Cardiff solicitor Leo Abse, older brother of poet and author Dannie Abse and Labour MP for Pontypool, is pictured at Cardiff General Railway Station as he left for the House of Commons, April 1961.

Pictured together at a poetry reading at the Chapter Arts centre in May 1980 are Cardiff-born poet Dannie Abse, left, and R.S. Thomas, who are ranked among the greatest poets of the 20th century.

Local Conservative candidate Terry Roche gets his message across to two of his supporters in the docks area of the city, December 1962.

Councillor Terry Roche is seen here on Corporation Road, Grangetown, with local residents, who were petitioning for a zebra crossing to be put across the road near Grange Gardens, September 1970.

David Llewellyn, prospective Conservative candidate, is seen here talking to Gabalfa housewife Mrs T.A. McLean, whose two children, Carol and Larraine, appear to be more interested in the *Western Mail & Echo* photographer, November 1949.

A wave from the victorious Conservative candidate for Cardiff North Mr David Llewellyn, later Sir David, after the result was declared at Cardiff City Hall in October 1951.

A shield bearing an artist's impression of the Cardiff Coat of Arms, which formed part of the Corporation decorations in Parliament Square, London, was purchased by David Llewellyn MP and presented by him to the city. Also seen in the picture are the Lord Mayor, Sir James Collins, with (left to right): Mrs R.H. Williams, Mrs David Llewellyn with Robert and Emma, Alderman George Ferrier, Mr David Llewellyn, the Lady Mayoress, Lady Collins, Mr W.G. Hopkins and Mr R.H. Williams, September 1953.

James Callaghan MP, the Chancellor of the Exchequer and MP for Cardiff South East, officially opened the Butetown Youth Centre in Loudoun Square on 17 December 1965, watched by the Lord Mayor, Alderman Mrs Miriam Bryant.

Members of the *Western Mail* panel of experts who decided the winner of the Sportsman of the Year award of 1961. Pictured from left to right are J.B.G. Thomas, sports editor, Lt-Col. Harry Llewellyn of Foxhunter fame, former boxer Jack Petersen and former cricketer Wilfred Wooler.

Cardiff entertainer Stan Stennett outside Buckingham Palace with his MBE. Pictured from left to right are his son Ceri, his wife Elizabeth and son Roger, March 1979.

John Parkman, former co-ordinator of the Wales Regional Crime Squad, received the MBE at Buckingham Palace in 1971.

John Parkman surrounded by his colleagues at the South Wales Constabulary Social Club on the occasion of his retirement after 33 years in the police force, 1970.

Arthur Manley, JP, of Highfields, Llandaff, with his wife as he visited Buckingham Palace to receive the MBE, 12 March 1963.

Norman Lloyd-Edwards, centre, now Sir Norman Lloyd-Edwards, the Conservative candidate, arrives with some of his supporters to cast their votes at the polling station in Colchester Avenue, June 1970.

On his final day as editor of the *Western Mail* John Rees was granted a privilege accorded to few journalists: he pressed the button to start the printing presses rolling. He is watched by his wife Ruth and Mr Robert Tyldesley, managing director of *Western Mail & Echo* Ltd, and his wife Cynthia, December 1987.

Marking the end of his six years as editor of the *Western Mail*, John Rees examines the paper for the last time, watched by his wife Ruth and managing director Robert Tyldesley, December 1987.

A civic farewell to John Rees, editor of the *Western Mail*, was given by the Lord Mayor, Councillor Julius Hermer, and his wife the Lady Mayoress Gloria Hermer. Pictured on the extreme left is Mrs Sybil Rich and on the extreme right her husband Mr Geoff Rich, editor of the *South Wales Echo*, December 1987.

Former *South Wales Echo* news editor Graham Bailey, who worked for nearly two decades heading up Cardiff City Council's public relations department, was presented with a gift on behalf of his colleagues by former *Echo* journalist Alan Michael, MP for Cardiff South and Penarth. Council chief executive Roger Paine is seen to the left of the photograph, January 1992.

Bob Yoder, 15, from California, takes a photograph of his great aunt, Cardiff's new Lord Mayor, Alderman Mrs Winifred Mathias, with relatives, friends and the city's mace bearers outside the city hall. They all made the trip from the US and Canada to see Mrs Mathias installed as the capital's first citizen, May 1972.

Cardiff-born businessman Norman Harvey with his pet lioness Sheba in his car showrooms on Penarth Road, May 1972.

'Vote For Jenkins'. Harry Parfitt, the well-known Cardiff scrap dealer, gives Councillor Jenkins a lift to the polling station, December 1959.

The Lord Mayor of Cardiff, Alderman J.H. Morgan, and Dr Loeff Burgomaster of s-Hertogenbosh, Holland, followed by the Lady Mayoress, Mrs J.H. Morgan, arrive at Llandaff Cathedral for the dedication of the memorial chapel to the 53rd Welsh Infantry (TA), April 1958.

Dorothy Penn, of Tremorfa, and Don Skene, of Llanrumney, cutting their wedding cake at St Margaret's Church, Roath, April 1956. Mr Skene was a well-known Welsh track cyclist and Empire Games bronze medallist.

Pictured at the launch of a book about old Barry town is famous Welsh author Gwyn Thomas, who wrote the foreword to the book. Seen from left to right are author Brian Luxton, Gwyn Thomas, David Stephens and Geoff Rich, editor of the *South Wales Echo*, 1977.

Five members of the North family, who retired as directors of the Cardiff building firm J. North and Sons (Builders) Ltd in 1989. Pictured from left to right are brothers Alf, 67, Len, 63, Derek, 57, Ken, 67, and Cliff, 65. On the left of the photograph is the leaded stained-glass office window, which at that time dated back 65 years.

Jack North (seated), founder of North & Sons Builders, is seen here with his two sons John Henry North (left) and Alfred Stanley North (right), c.1920.

Pope John Paul II made his first ever papal visit to Wales in 1982 and is seen here in his famous Popemobile at Pontcanna Fields.

Some of the guests at the Aberflyarff RFC bash at the city hall take time away from the revelry for a photograph. Seen from left to right are Olympic gold medallist Lynn Davies, rugby writer David Parry-Jones, Robert Tyldesley, managing director of the *Western Mail & Echo*, Geoff Rich, editor of the *South Wales Echo* and Wales wing Ken Jones. Pictured centre with the rugby ball is the famed *Echo* cartoonist Gren, who started it all.

Field Marshal Viscount Montgomery carrying out an inspection at the opening of the Douglas Haig Memorial Homes at Rumney, Cardiff. With him is Major T. Ifor Jones (chairman of the house committee), November 1953.

Nelson Mandela was made a freeman of Cardiff on his historic visit to the city in 1998. Seen in the left of the photograph is the Lord Mayor, Russell Goodway.

Julie Mosley receiving her Duke of Edinburgh gold award from the Lord Mayor Max Phillips and Lady Mayoress in the city hall, 1997.

The Lord Mayor, Councillor Victor Riley, with pupils of Severn Grove Junior School, Canton, in 1993. The pupils were presented with the Lord Mayor's Civic Award Certificate.

Mayoral Greeting. Controversial *South Wales Echo* journalist Dan O'Neill (left) with Lady Mayoress Val Swinburne, Lord Mayor Ricky Ormonde and the Cuban Ambassador to Britain Maria Florez (seated) in the Lord Mayor's parlour in the city hall, 1994.

The well-known Crwys Road butcher Ken Hutchings gets in celebratory mood for the 1977 Silver Jubilee celebrations.

CHAPTER SEVEN
WESTERN MAIL & ECHO

In this chapter we meet some of the people who worked on the *Western Mail* – Wales's national daily newspaper – and the *South Wales Echo*, an evening paper which at one time published six or seven editions throughout the day, but which is now printed at night and is available first thing in the morning.

In the early 1950s, the papers were produced by the old hot metal method; however, with the transfer of ownership from Thomson to Trinity the papers not only saw the move from broadsheet to tabloid, but also the introduction of new technologies.

The following photographs will give the reader a glimpse of some of those changes and the staff who enabled them.

Half a century at the *Western Mail*. Mr Ivor Mackenzie Thomas, manager of the printing department of *Western Mail & Echo* Ltd, presenting cheques on behalf of the directors C.R. Crawley and A. Hayes, who have completed 50 years of service at the Tudor Printing Works. Also seen in the photograph is Mr T.H. David (manager of the Tudor Works), December 1931.

The *South Wales Echo's* composing department's annual outing to Bristol Zoo in 1939. Left to right are Harry Dacey, Fred Archer (Father of Chapel), Dai Phillips (Overseer), Jock Wilson (Stereo Department), Ivor Hawkins (Chief Stonehand) and George Crawley.

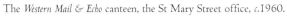

The *Western Mail & Echo* canteen, the St Mary Street office, *c*.1960.

The bill poster machine that used to be in the St Mary Street office.

Jobbing Advert Department, St Mary Street office *c.*1950. Pictured from left to right are Mervyn Ostler, Jack Relph, Ernie Hope and Ray Jones, while Mike Sheppard is seen standing.

Ivor Suller (left) shares a joke with managing director Mr Robert Tyldesley and Lord Kenneth Thomson, whose father, Lord Roy Thomson, opened the new Thomson House Building in Park Street on 20 June 1961.

Charlie Lewis seen at his linotype machine in the St Mary Street office, c.1960.

The editorial room, St Mary Street office, 1958.

Compositor Frank Young, who is setting the type, is being watched by Don Rowlands, editor of the *Western Mail* from 1959 to 1964, and night manager Chris Godwin, St Mary Street office, *c*.1960.

Compositors making up the pages, St Mary Street office, *c*.1960.

The legendary *Western Mail* boxing correspondent Alan Wood (left) gives the compositors a helping hand, *c*.1960.

Stereotyper Harry Were places the paper mâché matrix on to the made-up typeface to make a mould of the page, which was then cast as plates in the stereo department, c.1960.

From left to right are stereotyper Bob Potter, author Brian Lee and stereotypers Lenny Johnson and Jimmy Green. Seated in front is Bill Suter. This photograph was taken in the Park Street building in the 1970s.

Chief overseer Len Smith (left) with *South Wales Echo* composing room overseer Ivor Suller, January 1962.

Managing director David Thomas presents Ivor Suller with his long service award on 4 December 1972. Mr Suller died in 2009 aged 90.

Managing director David Thomas presented all of these *Western Mail & Echo* workers with their long service awards. Pictured on the extreme left is machine minder George Pearce, while in the centre is machine room assistant Ted Perryman, 4 December 1972.

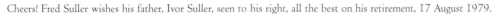

Cheers! Fred Suller wishes his father, Ivor Suller, seen to his right, all the best on his retirement, 17 August 1979.

'I'll drink to that', says Ivor Suller to his son Fred, 17 August 1979.

The new computerised composing room, Thomson House, 1979.

The end of an era. *South Wales Echo* editor Geoff Rich, wearing the white shirt, presses the button to start the printing presses with the last hot metal cast plates, as production manager Jim Savage looks on over his shoulder, 1980.

Henry Reynolds, who was in charge of the reading department at Thomson House, c.1975.

Composing room staff send Jack Wiltshaw on his way, c.1975.

Western Mail & Echo tele-ads girls present composing room manager George Codd with a birthday surprise.

This photograph was taken in the old St Mary Street office sometime in the 1950s. Among those in the picture are Jack Relph, Tom Bevan, Jack Parker, Godfrey Collins, Reg Jones, Charlie Lewis and Mike Sheppard.

Four *Western Mail & Echo* employees receive long service awards from managing director Duncan Currall. Pictured from left to right are sports journalist Karl Woodward, deputy chief sub editor Richard Alder, advertising co-ordinator Fred Suller and deputy pre-press manager Malcolm Hope.

Four *Western Mail & Echo* compositors who made the headlines when they were delayed 36 hours at the end of their holiday, at Moscow Airport. From left to right are Fred Suller, Vince Roles, Ernie Greenfield and Steve Walker.

This picture shows editors and departmental heads of the *Western Mail & Echo* when they gathered at the Royal Hotel on 15 November 1954 for a luncheon presentation marking the 70th birthday of managing director Sir Robert Webber, who is third from the left in the front row.

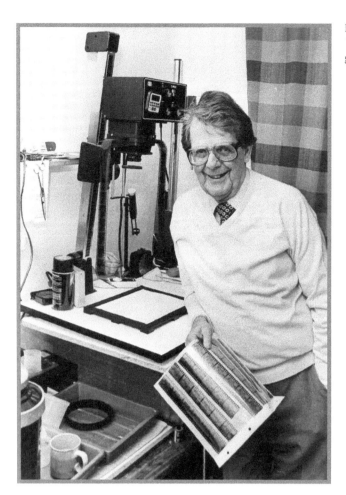

Rex Reynolds, a former chief assistant editor on the *Western Mail*, took up photography on his retirement and gained a Grade A pass in GCE O and A level.

South Wales Echo journalist Alec McKinty, pictured fourth from left, meets his penfriend Mrs Ana Carife and her husband Nei from Rio de Janeiro for the very first time in 17 years. Also in the picture are Alec's daughter Rachel, left, and his wife Cynthia, extreme right, 1986.

CHAPTER EIGHT
LEISURE AND ENTERTAINMENT

Over the years many famous people have visited Cardiff, among them several Hollywood film stars. Peter Lorre, the Hungarian-born actor who starred with Humphrey Bogart in the legendary film *Casablanca*, trod the boards at the New Theatre.

There are also those entertainers who come from within Cardiff itself, like Stan Stennett. Stan had his first big break when he won a talent competition at Newport Pavilion Theatre in 1947. More than 60 years on and now in his 80s he is still treading the boards. Stan has done it all: musicals, variety shows, films, plays, radio, television, documentaries and pantomime. He has appeared on *Coronation Street*, *Crossroads*, *Jokers Wild*, *Casualty* and *Heartbeat*. He has also had his own television shows and was resident comedian on the popular *Black and White Minstrel Show*. He has turned his hand to directing and producing and has shared the stage with Bob Hope, Mickey Rooney, Morecambe and Wise, Des O'Connor, Ronnie Corbett and scores of other well-known show business stars.

Another versatile Cardiff entertainer is Wyn Calvin, dubbed the Clown Prince of Wales and the Welsh Prince of Laughter. Wyn started off in repertory theatre and has been a comedian, actor, television chat show host, newspaper columnist and, of course, one of the greatest pantomime dames ever. He worked with Sir Donald Wolfit, who once admitted to him that he was jealous of his Widow Twankey, a part the great actor would have loved to have played himself. Even the famed Sir Ian McKellen came to Wyn for advice on how to play the part! In 1989 he was elected King Rat of the Order of Water Rats, a show business fraternity and charity, the only Welsh 'king' there has ever been. Awarded an MBE for his tireless services to charitable causes in 1991, Wyn has also been presented with a British Music Hall Society lifetime achievement award.

In 1997 a plaque was placed on the house in Cowbridge Road where Ivor Novello was born. Alfred Martin (left) on whose house the plaque was displayed is photographed with Robert Ernest, stage director of the Orbit Theatre, and Frank Wooles (right), director of the Orbit Theatre, October 1997.

Ivor Novello as he was seen in Alfred Hitchcock's *The Lodger* (1926). A matinee idol, Novello was mostly known for his romantic songs and stage musicals.

Hollywood actor Peter Lorre, who was appearing at the New Theatre, signs the visitors' book in the Lord Mayor's parlour at the city hall, watched by the Lord Mayor Timothy James Ferguson (first left). Councillor W.N.J. Muston, the deputy Lord Mayor, and his wife are also pictured, July 1949.

Peter Lorre also took time off to visit the Ministry of Pensions hospital, Rookwood, and is seen chatting to J.H. Williams, of Ebbw Vale, a World War One Victoria Cross holder, July 1949.

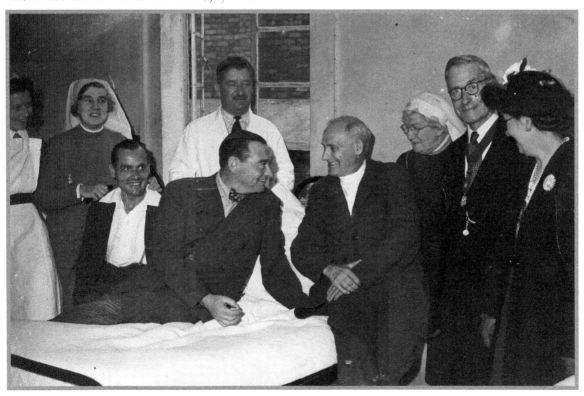

Cardiff's own show business entertainer 'Two Ton' Tessie O'Shea, December 1957.

Bill Owen, probably best known for his role as Compo in the long running television series *Last of the Summer Wine*, made a personal appearance at the Capitol Cinema in 1951. He is seen talking to W.F. Thomas, deputy chief constable of Cardiff, and Mrs Thomas, August 1951.

Cardiff-born singer Shirley Bassey and her daughters Sharon, 11, and Samantha, two, at London Airport before boarding a flight to Australia, 1966.

Hollywood actress Joan Rice, who turned down a film role to play at the Prince of Wales Theatre in 1958.

Welsh film actor Donald Houston enjoys a joke with members of the Angel Hotel staff. Pictured from the left are Rita Rees, Mary Dooley, Donald Houston, Ann Constantine and Paula Collings, May 1967.

Show business personality Harry Secombe with copies of his book *Twice Brightly* at a signing in Lears Bookshop on St Mary Street, October 1974.

Wyn Calvin, the Clown Prince of Wales, May 1983.

Dame Blodwen, alias Wyn Calvin, with some of the children from the charity Barnardos who attended a special dress rehearsal of *Jack and the Beanstalk* at the New Theatre, December 1988.

The comedian Danny Kaye is seen here being welcomed by the Lord Mayor upon his arrival at Cardiff Airport. He was making a personal appearance at the Sophia Gardens Pavilion. Pictured from left to right are Tom Davies, entertainments manager, Alderman J.H. Morgan, Danny Kaye, the Lady Mayoress Mrs Muston, the Lord Mayor Councillor W.H.J. Muston and Mr M.A. Hallam, the US Consul in Cardiff, July 1952.

South Wales Echo editor Geoff Rich (left), Judi Richards, general manager of the New Theatre and Alan Rustad, senior presenter of HTV's nightly news programme *Wales at Six*, introduce a new panel game, *First Things First*, in 1988.

Hollywood actress Gloria Swanson visited Cardiff in November 1950 for the Royal Command film performance of *The Mudlark*.

Gloria Swanson walks up the stairs with the manager of the Empire Cinema.

Another Hollywood film star who attended the preview was Montgomery Clift, seen here talking to broadcaster Leslie Mitchell.

The preview of Chwedl Nadolig Richard Burton – the Welsh version of that famous actor's *Christmas Story* – brought together members of the Burton family and Victor Spinetti, an old friend of the Burtons, at the Chapter Arts Centre. Pictured from the left are Verdun Jenkins (brother), Hilda Owen (sister), Victor Spinetti, Sian Owen, Davey Jenkins (brother) and Cassie Jenkins (sister), December 1990.

Jane Phillips, the Cardiff puppeteer who formed her own company – The Caricature Theatre Company – with some of her puppets, 1963.

Mr Reg Phillips, manager of the New Theatre, gazes at the bill for the pantomime *Red Riding Hood*, December 1961.

Cardiff opera singer Stuart Burrows, 1983.

Cardiff journalist John Cosslett, aged 24, shows off his recently bought 1932 Rolls-Royce in St Mary Street, Cardiff. John, who later became night editor of the *Western Mail*, is the author of *History Behind The Headlines* – the story of the *Western Mail* and its newspapers.

Lord Mayor Sir Charles Hallinan signals the start of the *Western Mail* International Welsh Car Rally, May 1976.

Famous Welsh author Jack Jones (1884–1970), who lived in the Whitchurch area of Cardiff for many years.

South Wales Echo journalist Alec McKinty examines a dalek, all in the name of duty, in December 1964. Alec is the author of *The Father of British Airships — A biography of E.T. Willows.*

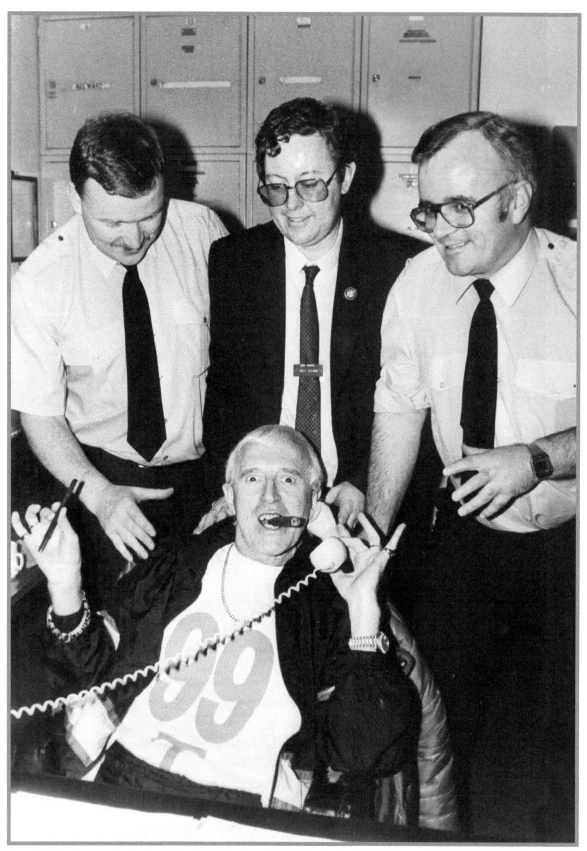

Jimmy Saville takes over the inquiry desk at the University of Wales Hospital in Cardiff. He was visiting the hospital to see his elder brother Vince. Pictured with Jimmy are Mark Loftus, Ray Evans and Tom Chiplin, January 1988.

Miss Cardiff, Leigh Robertson, 21, of Adamstown, is pictured with runner-up Francine Harris, 20, of Ely (left) and third-placed Geraldine Barrett, 20, of Canton, after winning her title at Ritzy's nightclub in Cardiff, June 1987.

Well-known Cardiff dancing teacher Kitty Slocombe is pictured just before she retired from her St Mary Street dance studio after 50 years. She is seen with two of her pupils, Mary Spiller, 33, of Dinas Powis (left) and Sally Lewis, 14, of Heath, 1985.

The Sybil Marks and Phil Williams Formation Dance team, pictured with the BBC Inter Regional Dancing Challenge Trophy, at a civic reception held for them at the city hall. Sybil Marks and Phil Williams hold the trophy aloft as members of the team look on, April 1958.

The members of the Sybil Marks Formation Dance team who represented Wales against the Home Counties in the BBC's television programme *Come Dancing*, January 1971.

Sybil Marks is seen holding the programme with some of the members of the Welsh team who reached the Final, April 1971.

Pictured before they left Cardiff for Germany, where they represented Great Britain in the European Championships, are members of the Sybil Marks Formation Dance team, October 1962.

Prison officer Patrick Stephens welcomes the Salvation Army musical group The Joy Strings to Cardiff Prison, c.1960.

Teenagers Helen Williams (left), of Roath, and Karen Western, of Canton, examine some of the exhibits at the David Morgan family store, which was celebrating its centenary, September 1969.

Parting gifts from members of staff were presented to Mr Clive Gerrard, general manager, and Mr Steve Thomas at the Howells staff dance on 1 June 1985. Pictured from left to right are Miss M. Clatworthy, Mrs Peggy Pinfield-Wells, Mrs Thomas, Miss A. Dickson, Mrs Gerrard and Miss K. Sanger.

With thoughts of the sun at Christmas are Mr and Mrs Jones, winners of Howells' holiday competition. Seen presenting their prize of a £400 holiday for two at a Christmas reception are Mr C. Gerrard, general manager, and Mr Gwyn Williams of Aspro Holidays, 1985.

270

D'ARC'S GRAND WAXWORK EXHIBITION,
ST. MARY STREET, CARDIFF.
FIGURES THAT MOVE LIKE LIFE.
10 A.M.—OPEN ALL THE YEAR ROUND.—10 P.M.
THE PLACE TO SPEND THAT IDLE HOUR.

Admission 5d. Including Tax. **Children 4d.**

D'arc's Grand Waxworks Exhibition first came to Cardiff in 1866. Later known as the Cardiff Continental Waxworks, it was situated at the Victoria Rooms at No. 90 St Mary Street. The entire contents of the show was sold off on 24 March 1946 and some of the exhibits ended up at Coney Beach, Porthcawl Amusement Park.

CHAPTER NINE
CITY OF ARCADES

Cardiff was once known as the city of arcades. The Royal Arcade, which dates back to around 1858, first opened with eight shops and a further 40 have been added over the years. The High Street Arcade was opened between 1887 and 1888 and was designed so that one could walk from the High Street to St John's Square, or St John's Street as it is correctly known.

Perhaps the best preserved of the Victorian arcades is Morgan Arcade, which was named after David Morgan, who opened a gentlemen's outfitters on The Hayes. The Wyndham Arcade was built in around 1887 and has never been as popular a venue as some of the other arcades in the city. Duke Street Arcade, built in 1902, leads into the High Street, while Dominions Arcade, situated on Queen Street, was built in 1921. Andrews Arcade and Oxford Arcade have now disappeared.

Castle Arcade, which runs from the High Street to Castle Street, was opened on 28 October 1885 by the Mayor Alderman David Jones. Many people will remember Bud Morgan's shop in the Castle Arcade. A Cardiff boy, who lost his right hand in a tramcar accident in 1928, Morgan became famous for his model aeroplanes. He was often seen in Llandaff fields flying the aeroplanes he manufactured. It has been said that he was a keen photographer who took hundreds of pictures of old Cardiff which have yet to be released.

The entrance to Castle Arcade in July 1965. Note the trolleybus wires.

Castle Arcade was renowned for its high skylights and picturesque balustraded balconies. In the 1980s, £50,000 was spent on new tiling and improved lighting.

Many Cardiffians will remember Bud Morgan's model aeroplane shop, seen on the right of this 1967 photograph of the Castle Arcade.

The Castle Arcade was built by Alderman Daniel Lewis from the plans of architect Peter Price. It underwent a £500,000 refurbishment in 1988. This photograph was taken in 1963.

Castle Arcade was opened by the Mayor of Cardiff, Alderman David Jones, on 28 October 1885. This photograph was taken in 1951.

These smart signs for Cardiff's arcades, produced by Cardiff City Council's Planning and Development Department, were part of Cardiff's contribution to the European Year of the Environment in 1987.

Morgan Arcade is named after David Morgan, who started out in business with a gentlemen's outfitters on The Hayes in 1879. This picture was taken in the 1960s.

Morgan Arcade was much busier when this photograph was taken in December 1986.

Duke Street Arcade was opened in 1902 and this photograph was taken some 60 years later.

Christmas time in Duke Street Arcade, 1986.

The Wyndham Arcade, with its glass roof supported on iron arches, was built in around 1887. This is how the St Mary Street entrance looked in April 1972.

There was talk at one time of demolishing the Wyndham Arcade, but there was nothing wrong with it when the *Western Mail & Echo* photographer took this photograph in November 1988.

These jubilant Wyndham Arcade traders celebrate the success of their campaign to save the arcade after plans to replace it with a new shopping complex were rejected. Pictured from left to right are Mike Point, Mike Servini, Benny Hardie, Neil and Angela Gillette, Julie Green and Les Skinner, May 1988.

There have been few betting shops in the arcades of Cardiff and the Ken Jones shop, situated in the Wyndham Arcade and pictured here in 1981, has been gone a long time. The arcade leads from St Mary Street to Mill Lane.

Dominions Arcade was opened in 1921 and leads from Queen Street to Greyfriars Road. It is seen here in October 1958.

The interior of the Dominions Arcade in October 1958.

The High Street Arcade, which was opened between 1880 and 1887, was designed so one could walk from the High Street to St John's Square. This photograph was taken c.1980.

The High Street Arcade was originally 50 yards long and had 34 shops with offices above. It is seen here in November 1980.

Queen Street Arcade, August 1971.

The old Queen Street Arcade which, like Andrews Arcade and Oxford Arcade, has since disappeared, November 1966.

The entrance to Andrews Arcade, which led from Queen Street to Crockherbtown Lane, c.1980. It was demolished just a couple of years ago.

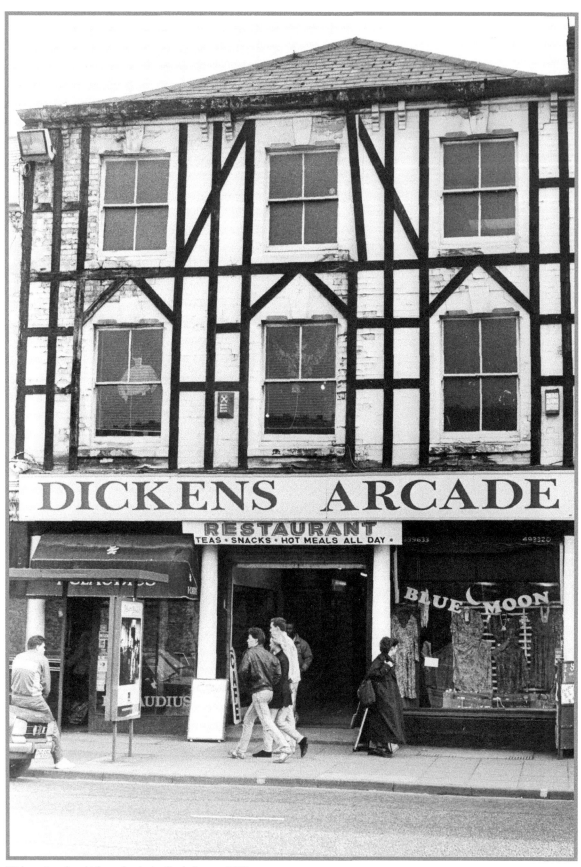

Dickens Arcade, which used to be in Castle Street, c.1989.

CHAPTER TEN
SPORTING MOMENTS

Many outstanding sportsmen and women have come from Cardiff and this chapter features a selection of them. Athlete Bernie Plain clocked up times for the 5,000m, 10,000m and the marathon more than 30 years ago that many of today's athletes would love to boast. At one stage in his illustrious career he held all the Welsh records from the 3,000m to the marathon. He lost out on a bronze medal at the 1974 European Games when he just failed to catch the great Gaston Roelants. A member of Cardiff Amateur Athletics Club, one memorable race he took part in was the 1973 AAA 10,000m at Crystal Palace, a race which saw Dave Bedford beat the legendary Ron Clark's world record. Bernie finished third and received an AAA Gold Medal award for his track performances in 1973. Three years later he won the then world's most famous marathon, the Polytechnic, in just over two hours and 15 minutes. He went on to win the race again in 1981 and finished second in 1983. Bernie ran 13 times for Britain and also represented Wales in nine world cross-country championships.

Another well-known Cardiff sportsman is cyclist Don Skene, who in 1954 represented Wales in the Vancouver Empire and Commonwealth Games, where he won a bronze medal in the 10-mile track event. At just 18, he was the youngest-ever cycling medallist and four years later, when the games were held at Cardiff, he won another bronze medal.

Cardiff-born Dame Tanni Grey-Thompson, one of the greatest Paralympians there has ever been, and world record 110m hurdler Colin Jackson are also featured.

Boxers Tommy Farr (left) and Giorgio Milo shake hands at the weigh-in at Sophia Gardens, before a fight which Farr won on points. In the centre is promoter Albert Davies, March 1957.

Cardiff middleweight boxer Phil Edwards was dubbed the Marlon Brando of Wales. This photograph was taken in 1957, the year he won all but one of his 10 fights.

Boxing manager Benny Jacobs (right) points out to *South Wales Echo* boxing critic Dave Phillips the danger spots on the gloves that badly injured Joe Erskine's eyes, September 1956.

Cardiff boxer Eddie Avoth raises his arms in victory after defeating John McCormack at the World Sporting Club in London. Around his waist he is wearing the Lonsdale belt he won after taking the British light heavyweight title in 1969.

Opposite: The much-loved Cardiff heavyweight boxer Joe Erskine, who died at the age of 56 in 1990.

A special testimonial evening was held at the Troubadour Club in Rover Way, Tremorfa, for boxer Glen Moody (left), who from 1930 to 1937 held the Welsh middleweight title. Former British heavyweight champion Jack Petersen lands a friendly punch on his chin, 1981.

The British featherweight champion Howard Winstone (right) signed a contract to fight Harry Carol of Cardiff at Maindy Stadium. Carol retired in the sixth round of the fight. Promoter Stan Cottle can be seen in the centre, 1962.

Olympic gold medallist Lynn Davies (right) presents Terry 'Slogger' Slocombe of St Albans baseball team with his award as Baseballer of the Year. Also in the photograph is Phil Haines, secretary of the Welsh National Baseball League, January 1967.

Paddy Hennessey of the Grange Albion team was awarded the Baseballer of the Year award at the annual presentations of the Welsh National Baseball League held at the Ocean Club, Tremorfa, on 1 December 1964. Officials Ted Peterson (right) and F. Burrowes, chairman of the English Baseball Association, admire the trophy.

Gill Miles (right) and Pam John, the Welsh pair bowling champions of 1991. They were also bronze medal winners at the Manchester British Commonwealth Games in 2002.

Cardiff City's most famous soccer captain Fred Keenor, who led the Bluebirds to their FA Cup victory over Arsenal in 1927, on a visit to Stacey Road Junior School in 1969.

Don Skene of Byways, Cardiff, is pictured winning the 550 yards cycling sprint at the Welsh Games at Maindy Stadium in 1961. Skene was a bronze medallist at the 1958 British Empire and Commonwealth Games.

Western Mail athletics correspondent Clive Phillips leaves Cardiff to cover the 19th Olympic Games in Mexico, October 1968. A former Welsh champion sprinter himself, Clive covered many big athletics championships during his time with the *Western Mail*.

Another great Welsh athlete: Colin Jackson (wearing number 12) of Cardiff AAC. He is seen here winning the 110m hurdles in the Pearl Assurance UK Championships at Cardiff Athletics Stadium, June 1990.

Dave Power of Australia, who pipped Wales's John Merriman (right) in the six-mile track race at the 1958 Empire and Commonwealth Games at Cardiff Arms Park.

Olympic long jump gold medallist Lynn Davies, seen on the left, with his coach Ron Pickering. The modest Davies has been a great ambassador for Wales.

Pictured at a training session of the Cardiff AAC at Maindy Stadium in May 1969 are, from left to right, Dennis Fowles, 18, Bernard Hayward, 20, Bob Maplestone, 22, and Paul Darney, 27. All four were Welsh international athletes and Maplestone, who moved to the US in 1970, was the first British athlete to run a four-minute mile indoors.

Cardiff's best-ever marathon runner Bernie Plain, seen on the left, and John Robertshaw complete their entry forms for the *Western Mail* marathon, 1982.

Jill Regan, 27, (right) of Heath, Cardiff, wins the 100 yards event at the eighth Cardiff May Day road races held around the civic centre in 1984.

At the city hall the Lord Mayor, Alderman Helena Evans, hands the baton and goodwill message to the 1948 Olympic Games marathon runner-up Tom Richards at the start of his run to Mountain Ash during the 1960 Nos Galan New Year's Eve Races.

Author Brian Lee, a member of Roath (Cardiff) Harriers, was granted the same honour four years later and Lord Mayor Alderman W.J. Hartland is about to send him off on his 20-mile run to Mountain Ash, New Year's Eve 1964.

Cardiff-born Jim Alford (left), who won the mile at the 1938 British Empire Games in Australia, is pictured with Steve Barry, who won the 30k walk at the 1982 Commonwealth Games in Brisbane in the record time of two hours, 10 minutes and 16 seconds, in 1987.

Cardiff AAC women's cross-country team won the European Championship Cup in Italy and were honoured with a civic reception in the city hall. Pictured after taking second place in the English Championships are Cardiff's point scorers Susan Tooby, Louise Copp, Kim Lock and Ann Roblin, 1984.

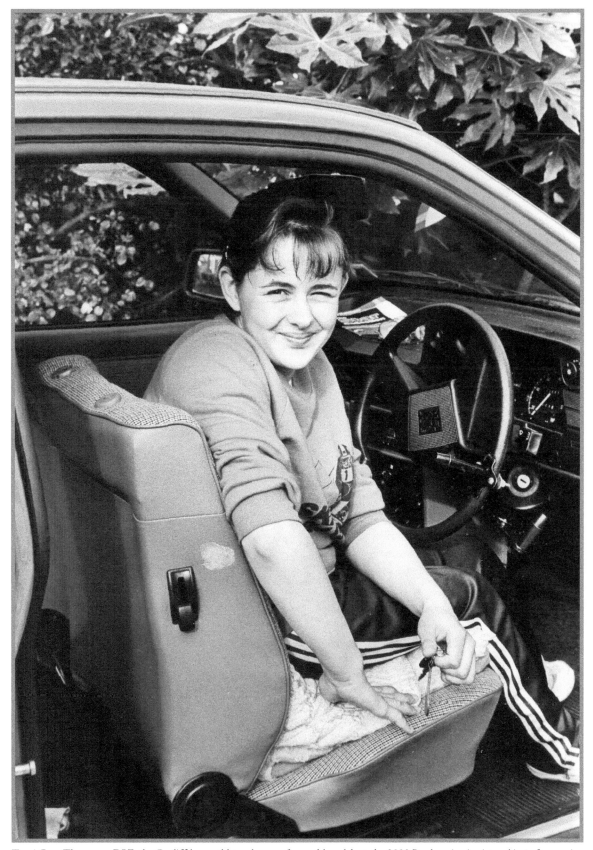

Tanni Grey-Thompson DBE, the Cardiff-born athlete who won four gold medals at the 2000 Paralympics, is pictured just after passing her driving test on her first attempt, July 1987.

The 1982 *Western Mail* marathon. Author Brian Lee, aged 46, can be seen wearing running number 32. Nearly 4,000 runners took part and Brian clocked up a time of three hours and 10 minutes.

Cardiff-born Tim Rooney winning the 1977 Horse & Hound Cup at Stratford on Mike Bishop's 50-1 outsider Devil's Walk, who was beaten in a photo finish in the same race the following year.

The cycling events at the 1958 British Empire and Commonwealth Games were held at Maindy Stadium. The Duke of Edinburgh is seen arriving by car.

Margaret Neale (left) presenting Joan Richards with the 1958 Welsh Intermediate Championship Trophy.

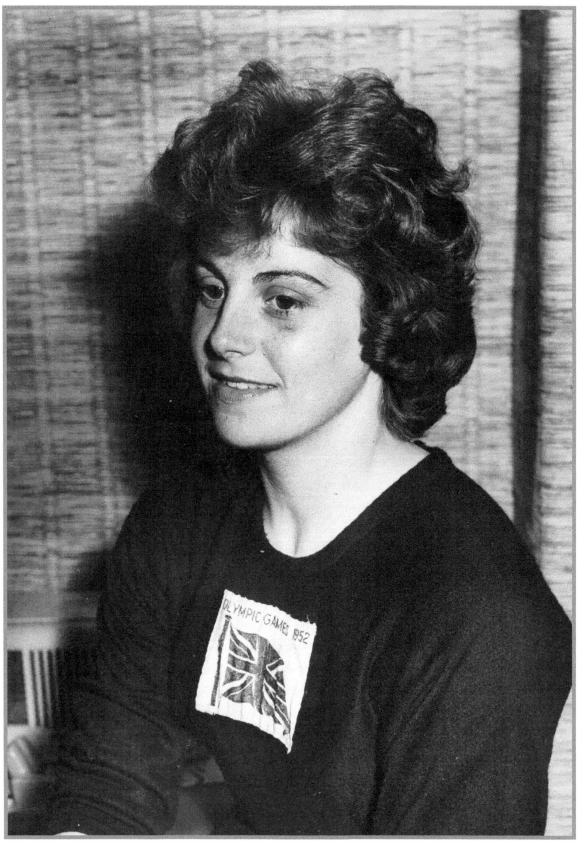

Gwynned Lingard, 25, of Clive Street, Grangetown, who was chosen for the British gymnastic team competing in the Rome Olympics in 1960.

The successful 1958 Cardiff Olympic gymnastic club team: Joan Richards, Daphne Ward, Carol Evans, Marion Rogers, Denise Goddard and Hazel Villiers.

Gymnasts Denise Goddard, 16, and Joan Richards, 20, practise for the British Gymnastic Championships at the Royal Albert Hall, February 1962.

Olympic gymnast Denise Goddard is presented with a travelling clock by Cardiff Olympic Ladies' Club, to take with her to the 1964 Tokyo Olympics.

Members of the Cardiff Olympic Ladies' Club with some of the awards won by the team, *c.*1960.

Budding champion gymnasts! The little girl with her hands on the shoulder of the gymnast in the front row is Karen Holland, daughter of Joan Richards, November 1976.

Surrounded by well-wishers, two Welsh gymnasts arrive at Cardiff General Station. From left to right can be seen Mr John Mulhall, Miss Denise Goddard and the Lord Mayor, Alderman W.J. Hartland, who welcomed their return to Wales after competing in the 1964 Tokyo Olympic Games.

Pictured at the 40th anniversary of the National Greyhound Racing Society celebration meeting at Cardiff Arms Park is Mrs A. Rabaiotti, who is presenting the Tito's Club Trophy to bookmaker Tommy Fish. He received the trophy on behalf of Mr W.D. Evans, owner of Red Wagon, who was the winner of the celebration week Inter-Track Cardiff versus Bristol 525 yards race, April 1968.

CHAPTER ELEVEN
CARDIFF'S FIREFIGHTERS

According to the fascinating *A History of The Cardiff City Fire Service*, 'it is in the year 1836 that mention is first made in the Cardiff Records of matters concerning the fire protection of the Borough as it was then.' The parochial records from St John the Baptist Church show that as far back as 1739 a manual fire engine was kept in the porch of the church tower. On Monday 1 February 1886 'the new steam fire engine ordered from Merryweathers and costing £700 was given a trial at the Canal, North Road. Before the trial in the town hall yard, in the presence of the Mayor, members of the town council and a considerable number of onlookers, the ceremony of naming the engine the *Walter Hemmingway* was performed by the Mayoress, who broke a bottle of champagne against it, expressing the hope that its services would but seldom be required.'

The Westgate Street Fire Station was opened in 1917 and was described thus: 'the lofty and imposing six-storey building was constructed of brick and concrete in Georgian style, with Portland stone dressings and was considered one of the finest elevations of its kind in the country. It covered an area of 5,600 square feet, had a frontage to Westgate Street of 140 feet and with its fine range of folding engine exit doors, its picturesque tiled roof, surmounted by a well designed tower overlooking the famous Cardiff Arms Park, was a striking example of what can be done to combine aesthetic lines with utilitarian requirements. The station occupied the site of the old river bed, which necessitated very deep foundations and a part was originally a pig market, acquired in 1828.'

The new Fire Services Headquarters and Central Fire Station were opened in Adam Street on 30 March 1973 by the Rt Hon. the Lord Mayor, Alderman Mrs Winifred Mathias.

Appliances are laid out in the Westgate Street Fire Station, shortly after it opened in 1917.

The headquarters of the fire brigade was in Westgate Street from 1917 until 1973.

Five Leyland fire appliances pictured in the civic centre, c.1928.

Cardiff Fire Brigade BO135 pictured in the Westgate Street yard, c.1930. The building in the background became known as Hodge House.

Cardiff Fire Brigade Dennis 'Big 4 Pump' KG5466, 1936.

Cardiff Fire Brigade Dennis/Merryweather 100ft turntable ladder CKG184, 1939. Note the firemen's living quarters above.

On display in the castle grounds just after the end of World War Two is the Cardiff Fire Brigade's No.7 CKG 178, which was affectionately known as 'The Old Lady'.

National Fire Service fireboat MV *Channel Fire* pictured in the Cardiff East Dock, 1942.

The MV *Haven Fire*, which was fitted out in Barry Dock and stationed there during the war before moving to Milford Haven. The suction hose can be seen on the roof of the deck house.

Fire engines turning out for a call from Westgate Street station, *c*.1962. The fireman is watching out for approaching traffic.

Photographed from the left are firemen George Elkins, Sid Brinning and Ted Stephens. The occasion was the retirement of last of the open body fire appliances at Westgate Street Fire Station, *c*.1950.

The 1968 Cardiff Fire Service Merryweather fire appliance with a 100ft turntable ladder.

During the war voluntary dock workers formed the Great Western Railway Fire Brigade. This photograph was taken on 17 June 1942.

ND - #0364 - 270225 - C0 - 276/195/12 - PB - 9781780913377 - Gloss Lamination